Understanding Dreams from God

Scott Breslin
&
Mike Jones

William Carey Library
Pasadena, California
www.WCLBooks.com

Understanding Dreams from God
Copyright © 2004 by Scott Breslin

Cover design by Joseph Gil

Scripture quotations are taken from the *Holy Bible, New International Version®, NIV ®*. Copyright © 1973, 1978, 1984 by International Bible Society. Used by permission of Zondervan Publishing House. All rights reserved.

All rights reserved. No part of this publication may be reproduced, stored in a retrieval system, or transmitted in any form or by any means—electronic, mechanical, photocopying, recording, or other—without the prior written permission of the publisher.

Published by William Carey Library Publishers
1605 E. Elizabeth Street
Pasadena, California 91104
www.WCLBooks.com

William Carey Library Publishers is a Ministry of the U.S. Center for World Mission, Pasadena, California.

Printed in the United States of America

ISBN: 0-87808-360-X (pbk.)

Contents

Preface 5

Introduction
   Why does God Speak through Dreams?................7

Chapter 1 To Turn from Wrongdoing
   The Dream of King Abimelech 9
   The Vision of Saul of Tarsus.............................12
   What is a Vision?..13
   Discussion Questions 17

Chapter 2 To Keep From Pride
   The Dream of King Nebuchadnezzar of Babylon..............19
   Discussion Questions 26

Chapter 3 To Preserve His Soul from the Pit
   The Vision of the Roman Centurion Cornelius..............28
   The Vision of the Disciple Peter 30
   Discussion Questions 36

Chapter 4 To Preserve His Life from Perishing by the Sword
   The Dream of Pharaoh, King of Egypt................37
   Prophecy vs. Dream Interpretation....................39
   The Dreams of Joseph (Stepfather of Isa)..........41
   Discussion Questions 46

Chapter 5 How Can You Tell if a Dream is from God?
   Guidelines for Testing Dreams..........................47
   1. Understand that all dreams are not from God..............48
   2. Confirm the dream doesn't conflict with Scripture........54
   3. Consult with followers of Isa........................55

4. Discern the purpose of the dream 56
5. Nurture a willingness to obey God 57
Discussion Questions 62

Chapter 6   Responding to God's Revelation
God's Greatest Revelation 63
Isa's Claims about Himself 64
Isa's Miracles 70
Isa's Character 70
Isa's Resurrection 72
Discussion Questions 74

Preface

We all dream. As a matter of fact, clinical research estimates we spend up to ten percent of our lives dreaming. Most dreams are a natural function of the human mind while sleeping. Some dreams are extraordinary. Some of our extraordinary dreams may even be supernatural.

This is the English edition of *Understanding Dreams from God*, a book originally published in the Middle East. It was written to provide insight on what the Bible has to say about dreams from God. The idea to write this booklet was birthed ten years ago, when I found myself being asked to interpret the dreams of friends and acquaintances in the Middle East who were seeing Jesus in their dreams. I later learned that many were having similar experiences throughout the region as well as in other parts of the world. The people who told me their dreams never thought to look in the Bible for answers to their questions about dreams. It was to their joy and surprise to hear that the Old and New Testaments are loaded with stories about dreams, visions, and their meanings.

Practically all the popular dream books on the market are written from Hindu, New Age and/or parapsychology viewpoints. In contrast, *Understanding Dreams from God* was written to present a biblical worldview, a view that affirms the historicity and authority of the Bible. After all, the Bible acknowledges that God has used dreams and visions to communicate with humanity for thousands of years. These holy writings have a lot to say about supernatural revelation, interpretations, purposes and limits of dreams, false dreams and the reality of the spirit world. Together with my friend Mike Jones, we wrote this simple book for our friends in the Middle East who wanted to hear what the Bible says regarding dreams from God.

In this English edition, we decided to keep four Arabic terms in the text rather than use the English equivalents. We did this to remind the read that *Understanding Dreams from God* was originally written for a Middle East audience. We trust this decision will enhance your enjoyment of the book rather than distract you. If not, we can change it in the next printing. But from this point forward (except when directly quoting Scripture) we will use the following four Arabic terms:

- *"Tawrat"* is the Torah or Pentateuch (first five books of the Old Testament). In the footnotes, for simplicity, we classified the prophetic books (Job, Joel, and Daniel) as part of the Tawrat. Also spelt Tawraat, Taurat or Tevrat.
- *"Zabur"* is the Psalms of David. Sometimes spelt Zabin.
- *"Injil"* is the New Testament. The Tawrat, Zabur, and Injil (as well as the Koran) are considered authoritative holy books by most orthodox Muslims.
- *"Isa"* is the name for Jesus. Often you will see the title Sayyidna (our lord) placed before Isa (i.e. Sayyidna Isa) as a title of respect and honor in Arabic literature. For simplicity's sake we refer to Jesus Christ simply as Isa.

Understanding Dreams from God has already whetted the appetite of thousands who are seeking to understand the meaning of dreams and visions from God. As followers of Isa, we are grateful for the opportunity to share with you a unique perspective of *Understanding Dreams from God according to the Tawrat, Zabur, and Injil.*

Scott Breslin
August 2004

Introduction

In the past, God used dreams as an important method of communicating with humanity. Today, all over the world people from different religious backgrounds, cultures and social status are having extraordinary dreams. In preparation for writing this book, we have heard firsthand many extraordinary dreams from people all over the world. What we have witnessed is consistent with what one of the prophets of the Tawrat said long ago. It is written:

> *In the last days, God says, I will pour out my Spirit on all people. Your sons and daughters will prophesy, your young men will see visions; your old men will dream dreams.*[1]

Over the past few years we have studied the dreams and visions recorded in the Tawrat, Zabur and Injil. We have also interviewed large numbers of people who have had extraordinary dreams. We have summarized the highlights of our research in this booklet, *Understanding Dreams from God,* with the hope that it will shed light on many of your questions about dreams, including questions about your own dreams. It will:

- Introduce you to key dreams and visions in the Tawrat, Zabur and Injil (chapters 1-4)
- Suggest guidelines for understanding and testing dreams (chapter 5)
- Suggest how to respond to dreams from God (chapter 6)
- Facilitate small group meetings with discussion questions at the end of each chapter

---

[1] Tawrat - Joel 2:28 and Injil - Acts 2:17

If God has given you a dream, you can be sure he has something important to say to you. This booklet was written to help you understand what God might be saying. Let's start by asking a question.

Why Does God speak through Dreams?
The best way to answer this question is to look in the Tawrat. We read about a man named Elihu who understood that God communicates to humanity in various ways. He mentions four reasons why God sends dreams.

> *For God does speak--now one way, now another--though man may not perceive it. In a dream, in a vision of the night, when deep sleep falls on men as they slumber in their beds, he may speak in their ears and terrify them with warnings, to turn man from wrongdoing and keep him from pride, to preserve his soul from the pit, his life from perishing by the sword.*[2]

According to Elihu, God warns us through dreams in order to:

1) Turn man from wrongdoing
2) Keep him from pride
3) Preserve his soul from the pit
4) Protect him from death (or perishing by the sword)

Practically all of the dreams in the Tawrat and Injil serve one or more of these purposes. The four purposes of dreams listed above provide the outline of this book.

---

[2] Tawrat - Job 33:14-18

Chapter 1

To Turn from Wrongdoing

The first reason God gives dreams is to turn people from doing wrong. Such dreams often serve to minimize the negative effects of the dreamer's ignorance, prejudice, or pride. There are several dreams of this category in the Tawrat and Injil. We will look at two. The first story is about the dream of King Abimelech and comes from the Tawrat.

The Dream of King Abimelech:
Our first story takes place while Abraham (one of the great prophets) was traveling from region to region with his wife Sarah and their herds of sheep, goats and camels around 2090 BC. Eventually he entered into the city of Gerar where a powerful king named Abimelech ruled. Even though Abraham was a great prophet, he was also a man who could make mistakes.[3] In this case Abraham feared that King Abimelech, upon seeing Sarah's beauty, would kill him and take Sarah as his own wife. Therefore, Abraham and Sarah pretended to be brother and sister (in fact, Sarah was also Abraham's half-sister) when they finally met King Abimelech.

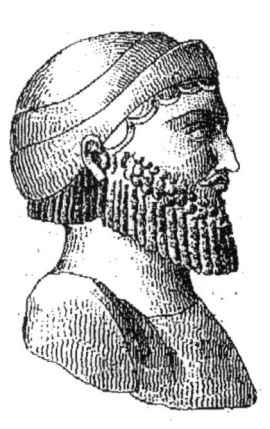

---

[3] The Tawrat does not present the prophets as perfect or flawless people. In fact, the entire Bible clearly teaches there is no such thing as a perfect or sinless human (with the exception of Isa). Therefore we should not be shocked that Abraham had human weaknesses even though he was a great man of God. In this story we get a glimpse of God's mercy as God rescues Sarah, Abraham and King Abimelech from the messy situation created by their own errors. God loves us even when we make a mess of our lives. His help and love for you isn't dependent on you being flawless but on God's mercy and grace.

The plan backfired and King Abimelech, seeing Sarah's beauty, took her into his harem, believing that she was Abraham's unmarried sister. Read the story for yourself and pay careful attention to King Abimelech's dream.

Now Abraham moved on from there into the region of the Negev and lived between Kadesh and Shur. For a while he stayed in Gerar, and there Abraham said of his wife Sarah, "She is my sister." Then Abimelech king of Gerar sent for Sarah and took her.

But God came to Abimelech in a dream one night and said to him, "You are as good as dead because of the woman you have taken; she is a married woman." Now Abimelech had not gone near her, so he said, "Lord, will you destroy an innocent nation? Did he not say to me, 'She is my sister,' and didn't she also say, 'He is my brother'? I have done this with a clear conscience and clean hands." Then God said to him in the dream, "Yes, I know you did this with a clear conscience, and so I have kept you from sinning against me. That is why I did not let you touch her. Now return the man's wife, for he is a prophet, and he will pray for you and you will live. But if you do not return her, you may be sure that you and all yours will die."

Early the next morning Abimelech summoned all his officials, and when he told them all that had happened, they were very much afraid. Then Abimelech called Abraham in and said, "What have you done to us? How have I wronged you that you have brought such great guilt upon me and my kingdom? You have done things to me that should not be done." And Abimelech asked Abraham, "What was your reason for doing this?" Abraham replied, "I said to myself, 'There is surely no fear of God in this place, and they will kill me because of my wife.' Besides, she really is my sister, the daughter of my father though not of my mother; and she became my wife. And when God had me wander from my father's household, I said to her, 'This is how you can show your love to me: Everywhere we go, say of me, "He is my brother."' Then Abimelech brought sheep and cattle and male and female slaves and gave them to Abraham, and he returned Sarah his wife to him. And Abimelech said, "My land is before you; live wherever you like." To Sarah he said, "I am giving your brother a thousand shekels of silver. This is to cover the offense against you before all who are with you; you are completely vindicated." Then Abraham prayed to God, and God healed Abimelech, his wife and his slave girls so they could have children again, for the LORD had closed up every womb in Abimelech's household because of Abraham's wife Sarah.[4]

Even though the King Abimelech had sinned,[5] God showed him mercy before he made the matter even worse. The dream

---

[4] Tawrat - Genesis 20
[5] Even though King Abimelech took Sarah with a "clear conscience" it didn't make him innocent of sin. His blaming Abraham for saying "she is my sister" was not a satisfactory excuse in God's eyes. King Abimelech's lust for women and an 'above-the-law' attitude convinced him to "take" whatever he wanted (without permission from God or man). Thus, the

was a warning to keep the king from further wrongdoing, not a declaration of his innocence.

A complicated problem was resolved without severe consequences. The king repented, returned Sarah and even paid a settlement to Abraham. Abraham prayed a blessing upon King Abimelech so that the matter was completely settled.

The Vision of Saul of Tarsus: Our next story is about how a man named Saul of Tarsus changed from being a persecutor of God's people into one of their great leaders. Saul was a Jewish religious teacher. He was extremely proud of his religious training, traditions and ancestry. Saul was so enthusiastic to protect the Jewish religious traditions that he found himself working against God rather than for him. Isa warned his disciples that they would be victims of such people when he told them:

> ... *a time is coming when anyone who kills you will think he is offering a service to God.*[6]

Saul of Tarsus was just such a man as described by Isa. The story of Saul's vision is recorded in the Injil. It takes place around 35 AD not long after Isa had ascended to heaven. The Jewish religious authorities were persecuting many of the

---

dream God gave King Abimelech was an act of mercy to keep him from further wrongdoing.
[6] Injil - John 16:2

followers of Isa. They felt threatened by the teachings of Isa propagated by his followers. The Jewish religious authorities vigorously attempted to destroy the growing religious community that Isa had started among the Jews. Thousands of Jews were following the teachings of Isa in a reform

---

What is a Vision?
Dreams and visions are very similar. The best way to make a distinction between the two is to think of a dream as a vision that happens when asleep. Visions can happen when you are asleep or awake. There are different types of visions. In a vision your eyes may be open or closed. A vision may take place in the mind or through the eyes and ears. When someone has a vision other people nearby will not necessarily see or hear the vision. Saul's vision was very real but his traveling companions only heard sounds; they didn't see anyone.

---

movement that was being called "The Way." But the chief priests considered it a sect and a threat to their authority. Therefore they selected a zealous conservative Jew named Saul to arrest and persecute the followers of Isa. Saul believed that by persecuting the members of this "sect" he was "offering a service to God." Saul went from town to town with a group of soldiers arresting those who followed the teachings of Isa. Saul was ruthless and effective. The Injil describes the story of Saul's vision:

> *Meanwhile, Saul was still breathing out murderous threats against the Lord's disciples. He went to the high priest and asked him for letters to the synagogues in Damascus, so that if he found any there who belonged to the Way, whether men or women, he might take them as prisoners to Jerusalem. As he neared Damascus on his journey, suddenly a light from*

> *heaven flashed around him. He fell to the ground and heard a voice say to him, "Saul, Saul, why do you persecute me?" "Who are you, Lord?" Saul asked. "I am Jesus, whom you are persecuting," he replied. "Now get up and go into the city, and you will be told what you must do." The men traveling with Saul stood there speechless; they heard the sound but did not see anyone. Saul got up from the ground, but when he opened his eyes he could see nothing. So they led him by the hand into Damascus. For three days he was blind, and did not eat or drink anything.[7]*

God used a vision to "open" Saul's eyes. For the first time Saul realized his efforts to persecute followers of Isa were wrong. Saul's prejudice and ignorance had blinded him to God's purposes. Saul learned that the followers of Isa were God's friends and to persecute them was the same as persecuting Isa himself. What Saul had meant for good had really been very evil. Saul had been fighting against God's people. This was terrifying news for a man who had dedicated his life to pleasing God. The story continues with another vision. This time God gives a vision to a disciple of Isa named Ananias.

> *In Damascus there was a disciple named Ananias. The Lord called to him in a vision, "Ananias!" "Yes, Lord," he answered. The Lord told him, "Go to the house of Judas on Straight Street and ask for a man from Tarsus named Saul, for he is praying. In a vision he has seen a man named Ananias come and place his hands on him to restore his sight." "Lord,"*

---

[7] Injil - Acts 9:1-9

> *Ananias answered, "I have heard many reports about this man and all the harm he has done to your saints in Jerusalem. And he has come here with authority from the chief priests to arrest all who call on your name." But the Lord said to Ananias, "Go! This man is my chosen instrument to carry my name before the Gentiles and their kings and before the people of Israel. I will show him how much he must suffer for my name."*[8]

Notice that when Isa appeared to Ananias in the vision, Ananias immediately recognized Isa. Unlike Saul, Ananias didn't ask, "Who are you?" but answered, "Yes, Lord." Ananias knew Isa because he was one of his followers. Obviously Saul had a dangerous reputation among the followers of Isa. Yet Ananias obeyed his Lord and not his fear. The story continues:

> *Then Ananias went to the house and entered it. Placing his hands on Saul, he said, "Brother Saul, the Lord--Jesus, who appeared to you on the road as you were coming here--has sent me so that you may see again and be filled with the Holy Spirit." Immediately, something like scales fell from Saul's eyes, and he could see again. He got up and was baptized, and after taking some food, he regained his strength. Saul spent several days with the disciples in Damascus. At once he began to preach in the synagogues that Jesus is the Son of God.*[9] *All those who heard him were astonished and asked, "Isn't he the*

---

[8] Injil - Acts 9:10-16
[9] The term "Son of God" is used in a metaphoric sense. It does not mean that Jesus is the biological child of God.

man who raised havoc in Jerusalem among those who call on this name? And hasn't he come here to take them as prisoners to the chief priests?" Yet Saul grew more and more powerful and baffled the Jews living in Damascus by proving that Jesus is the Christ. After many days had gone by, the Jews conspired to kill him, but Saul learned of their plan. Day and night they kept close watch on the city gates in order to kill him. But his followers took him by night and lowered him in a basket through an opening in the wall. When he came to Jerusalem, he tried to join the disciples, but they were all afraid of him, not believing that he really was a disciple.[10]

This is a wonderful story of how God used a dream (or in this case, a vision) to turn a person from wrongdoing. God gave Saul the opportunity to turn from his sin, repent and respond in obedience to his revelation. As a result, Saul not only stopped persecuting the followers of Isa but he also joined them. He was eventually accepted by the other disciples and in a few years became a great teacher and leader among Isa's followers. There is a lot written about Saul in the Injil, but he is better known by the name Paul.

---

[10] Injil - Acts 9:17-26

Discussion Questions

1. How did Abraham's fear set the stage for King Abimelech's dream?

2. Describe how King Abimelech's dream turned him from doing wrong.

3. Describe how Saul's attitude changed after his dream.

4. What were the similarities between King Abimelech and Saul's response to their dream/vision?

5. Why do you think God gave Saul a second chance instead of punishment?

6. What can we learn about God's character from these two dreams?

7. Have you had or heard of a dream that turned a person from wrongdoing?

Chapter 2

To Keep from Pride

Another purpose of God-given dreams mentioned in the Scripture[11] is to 'keep people from pride.' The Tawrat, Zabur and Injil teach that God opposes the proud.

> *... All of you, clothe yourselves with humility toward one another, because, "God opposes the proud but gives grace to the humble."*[12]

A person filled with pride is primarily concerned about himself and not about God or others. Pride therefore births all sorts of other evils. God gives dreams to keep people from pride.

The Dream of King Nebuchadnezzar of Babylon: This dream took place during the reign of King Nebuchadnezzar of Babylon (605-562 BC). He ruled the Babylonian Empire at the height of its strength and power. The Babylonian Empire had become one of the richest and most powerful empires the world had ever seen. King Nebuchadnezzar completely conquered the Jewish Kingdom of Judah. The Jewish survivors were exiled and resettled in Assyria and Babylon or left in poverty under the rule of Babylonian governors. King Nebuchadnezzar ruled the civilized world of his day. He took great pride in being the most powerful man on earth. His pride was so great he had

---

[11] Tawrat - Job 33:14-18
[12] Injil - 1 Peter 5:5

himself worshipped as a god. Things changed one night when he had a dream that made him afraid. Below is the story from the Tawrat.

These are the visions I saw while lying in my bed: I looked, and there before me stood a tree in the middle of the land. Its height was enormous. The tree grew large and strong and its top touched the sky; it was visible to the ends of the earth. Its leaves were beautiful, its fruit abundant, and on it was food for all. Under it the beasts of the field found shelter, and the birds of the air lived in its branches; from it every creature was fed.

In the visions I saw while lying in my bed, I looked, and there before me was a messenger, a holy one, coming down from heaven. He called in a loud voice: 'Cut down the tree and trim off its branches; strip off its leaves and scatter its fruit. Let the animals flee from under it and the birds from its branches. But let the stump and its roots, bound with iron and bronze, remain in the ground, in the grass of the field. Let him be drenched with the dew of heaven, and let him live with the animals among the plants of the earth. Let his mind be changed from that of a man and let him be given the mind of an animal, till seven times pass by for him. The decision is announced by messengers, the holy ones declare the verdict, so that the living may know that the Most High is sovereign over the kingdoms of men and gives them to anyone he wishes and sets over them the lowliest of men.

> *This is the dream that I, King Nebuchadnezzar, had.*[13]

King Nebuchadnezzar was very troubled by the dream. His large staff of magicians, astrologers and diviners was called to his palace but none of them could explain the meaning of his dream. Finally King Nebuchadnezzar called for the Prophet Daniel, a man who loved and worshiped the true God. Daniel was unlike the other advisors of the king who worshiped idols and practiced divination. Many years earlier, when Daniel was only a youth, the previous king of Babylon had captured Jerusalem and taken Daniel as a slave. But because Daniel showed promise, he was trained in the king's palace and given the Babylonian name of "Belteshazzar." He served as an advisor to King Nebuchadnezzar and had the reputation of being a man of God. The story continues as the king explains his dream to Daniel.

> *Then Daniel (who was also called Belteshazzar) was greatly perplexed for a time, and his thoughts terrified him. So the king said, "Belteshazzar, do not let the dream or its meaning alarm you." Belteshazzar answered, "My lord, if only the dream applied to your enemies and its meaning to your adversaries! The tree you saw, which grew large and strong, with its top touching the sky, visible to the whole earth, with beautiful leaves and abundant fruit, providing food for all, giving shelter to the beasts of the field, and having nesting places in its branches for the birds of the air--you, O king, are that tree! You have become great and strong; your greatness has*

---

[13] Tawrat - Daniel 4:10-18

grown until it reaches the sky, and your dominion extends to distant parts of the earth. "You, O king, saw a messenger, a holy one, coming down from heaven and saying, 'Cut down the tree and destroy it, but leave the stump, bound with iron and bronze, in the grass of the field, while its roots remain in the ground. Let him be drenched with the dew of heaven; let him live like the wild animals, until seven times pass by for him.' This is the interpretation, O king, and this is the decree the Most High has issued against my lord the king: You will be driven away from people and will live with the wild animals; you will eat grass like cattle and be drenched with the dew of heaven. Seven times will pass by for you until you acknowledge that the Most High is sovereign over the kingdoms of men and gives them to anyone he wishes. The command to leave the stump of the tree with its roots means that your kingdom will be restored to you when you acknowledge that Heaven rules. Therefore, O king, be pleased to accept my advice: Renounce your sins by doing what is right, and your wickedness by being kind to the oppressed. It may be that then your prosperity will continue."[14]

Daniel displayed great courage interpreting this dream about Nebuchadnezzar's downfall. It wasn't politically correct to warn a king about the downfall of his reign. Daniel could have lost his head for speaking so plainly to the king. Yet, in spite of the risk, Daniel warned the king to renounce his sins, to be kind to the oppressed and to acknowledge God as the

---

[14] Tawrat - Daniel 4:19-27

Most High Sovereign. But the warning went unheeded and the king did not repent of his excessive pride. He did not change his ways. He did not acknowledge God as the Most High Sovereign. The story continues:

> *All this happened to King Nebuchadnezzar. Twelve months later, as the king was walking on the roof of the royal palace of Babylon, he said, "Is not this the great Babylon I have built as the royal residence, by my mighty power and for the glory of my majesty?" The words were still on his lips when a voice came from heaven, "This is what is decreed for you, King Nebuchadnezzar: Your royal authority has been taken from you. You will be driven away from people and will live with the wild animals; you will eat grass like cattle. Seven times will pass by for you until you acknowledge that the Most High is sovereign over the kingdoms of men and gives them to anyone he wishes." Immediately what had been said about Nebuchadnezzar was fulfilled. He was driven away from people and ate grass like cattle. His body was drenched with the dew of heaven until his hair grew like the feathers of an eagle and his nails like the claws of a bird.*

King Nebuchadnezzar had elevated himself to the position of a god. Yet God showed great patience and mercy when he gave Nebuchadnezzar both a dream and the prophet (Daniel) to interpret the dream. Yet his excessive pride caused him to ignore God's warning.

King Nebuchadnezzar ruled over thousands of people, controlled large armies, had incredible wealth, and was surrounded with great learning. Yet instead of thanking God and ruling justly, Nebuchadnezzar neglected his God-given responsibility to protect the poor in his kingdom. God cares for the poor and oppressed and appoints the rulers of the earth to treat them kindly. In his great pride Nebuchadnezzar neglected his duty to protect the oppressed and considered himself a god. The Tawrat tells us that God detests the proud.

> *The LORD detests all the proud of heart. Be sure of this: They will not go unpunished. Through love and faithfulness sin is atoned for; through the fear of the LORD a man avoids evil.*[15]

God's warning was an expression of his grace and kindness to Nebuchadnezzar. God does not enjoy punishing people any more than a father enjoys punishing his son. God is loving towards us. For it says in the Injil:

> *The Lord is not slow in keeping his promise, as some understand slowness. He is patient with you, not wanting anyone to perish, but everyone to come to repentance.*[16]

Yet in the end, after much unnecessary suffering (had he listened to Daniel's advice) King Nebuchadnezzar finally came to his senses.

> *At the end of that time, I, Nebuchadnezzar, raised my eyes toward heaven, and my sanity was restored. Then I praised the Most High; I honored and glorified him who lives forever. His dominion is an eternal dominion; his kingdom endures from generation to*

---

[15] Tawrat - Proverbs 16:5-6
[16] Injil – 2 Peter 3:9

generation. All the peoples of the earth are regarded as nothing. He does as he pleases with the powers of heaven and the peoples of the earth. No one can hold back his hand or say to him: "What have you done?" At the same time that my sanity was restored, my honor and splendor were returned to me for the glory of my kingdom. My advisers and nobles sought me out, and I was restored to my throne and became even greater than before. Now I, Nebuchadnezzar, praise and exalt and glorify the King of heaven, because everything he does is right and all his ways are just. And those who walk in pride he is able to humble.[17]

Even though King Nebuchadnezzar didn't initially respond to the revelation of his dream, God patiently waited for him to be humbled. In the end, Nebuchadnezzar came to his senses, raised his eyes towards heaven and glorified God as the Most High sovereign instead of himself. God's mercy is so great that even an arrogant and wicked man like King Nebuchadnezzar cannot wear out his patience and kindness.

---

[17] Tawrat - Daniel 4:18-37

Discussion Questions

1. Contrast the differences between King Nebuchadnezzar's dream and King Abimelech's dream from chapter 1.

2. Why do you think God hid the meaning of King Nebuchadnezzar's dream in symbolic imagery?

3. What advice did Daniel give King Nebuchadnezzar? Was it followed?

4. What did King Nebuchadnezzar finally learn at the end of his ordeal?

5. Why do you think God opposes the proud? Is humility something you value?

6. Are you proud?

7. What can we learn about God from this dream?

Chapter 3

To Preserve His Soul from the Pit

A third purpose of God-given dreams is to preserve people's souls from the pit.[18] In the Tawrat and Zabur the term 'pit' is often used metaphorically as death and/or the place of the dead. It is described as a deep, dark and lonely place (or state of existence) cut off and separate from the land of the living, a place to be avoided. God gives dreams to save souls from going to this "pit" or place of the dead.

This type of dream (or vision) typically points the dreamer in a different direction than where the dreamer was previously headed. In other words, this type of dream may cause a person to change his mind, seek advice, and/or seek a fuller understanding of God in places he wouldn't otherwise have looked. We can call these "pointing dreams" because they point the dreamer away from the "pit" and toward the path that leads to God. There are also several examples of this type of dream in the scriptures. This also was the most common category of dream that we heard in our interviews and research.

Our next story comes from the Injil and contains two examples of "pointing dreams." To better appreciate the significance of these dreams, there are a few things you should know about the Jewish culture and history of that period (around 35-40 AD). First, the lands of Palestine were controlled by the Roman Empire whose armies occupied the land and collected taxes. The Jews, for their part, were allowed to practice their religious traditions as long as they paid their taxes and submitted to Roman rule. Jews kept to

---

[18] Tawrat – Job 33:14-18

themselves and maintained a closed society. It was against Jewish culture to associate with Romans (or any non-Jew). Jewish religious tradition taught that entering a non-Jewish home made them ritually unclean and to eat with a non-Jew was forbidden.

In the beginning practically all of Isa's followers were Jewish. This created an interesting dilemma since no one is completely immune to the prejudices and misconceptions of one's own culture. In the case of Isa's followers, they could not understand that God loved non-Jews. Isa taught that God loved all people (both Jew and non-Jew) but his disciples had difficulty grasping this teaching. It stood in vivid contrast with the Jewish worldview of their day. It was forbidden to even eat with non-Jews. Yet, the last command Isa gave to his followers was to go into the entire world and spread the message of God's love to all people (Jew and non-Jew). Yet his followers were apparently so programmed by their customs they couldn't (or didn't) obey Isa's teaching about this. They were blinded by their prejudices.

The Vision of the Roman Centurion Cornelius: This story is about how God began to free the Jewish followers of Isa from their prejudice. Their customs were keeping them from obeying the command of God to go out into the entire world. This is also the story about how the teachings of Isa began to spread to non-Jews. The story involves two visions and two men. The first man is Cornelius, a non-Jew and a centurion in the Roman army. The second man is Peter, a Jewish follower of Isa and an important leader of Isa's disciples.

> *At Caesarea there was a man named Cornelius, a centurion in what was known as the Italian Regiment. He and all his family were devout and God-fearing; he gave generously to those in need and prayed to God regularly. One day at about three in the afternoon he had a vision. He distinctly saw an angel of God, who came to him and said, "Cornelius!" Cornelius stared at him in fear. "What is it, Lord?" he asked. The angel answered, "Your prayers and gifts to the poor have come up as a memorial offering before God. Now send men to Joppa to bring back a man named Simon who is called Peter. He is staying with Simon the tanner, whose house is by the sea." When the angel who spoke to him had gone, Cornelius called two of his servants and a devout soldier who was one of his attendants. He told them everything that had happened and sent them to Joppa.*[19]

Cornelius was probably an Italian since he was a centurion in the Italian Regiment, an elite regiment of Roman soldiers. Cornelius and his family were devout and God-fearing. They prayed and gave gifts to the poor. Yet being 'good' was not enough. They lacked important knowledge about God. Knowledge that was critical for true worship. God wanted Cornelius and his family to have a fuller understanding of the One they worshipped.

---

[19] Injil - Acts 10:1-8

The Vision of the Disciple Peter: The man Cornelius sent for was a Jewish follower of Isa named Peter. Peter had a fuller understanding of God than Cornelius. But remember, Jews didn't associate with Romans and they certainly didn't go to their homes to visit. Peter was about to have his values challenged. Was he going to obey God or the customs taught by his Jewish cultural heritage? The story continues:

About noon the following day as they were on their journey and approaching the city, Peter went up on the roof to pray. He became hungry and wanted something to eat, and while the meal was being prepared, he fell into a trance. He saw heaven opened and something like a large sheet being let down to earth by its four corners. It contained all kinds of four-footed animals, as well as reptiles of the earth and birds of the air. Then a voice told him, "Get up, Peter. Kill and eat." "Surely not, Lord!" Peter replied. "I have never eaten anything impure or unclean." The voice spoke to him a second time, "Do not call anything impure that God has made clean." This happened three times, and immediately the sheet was taken back to heaven.[20]

Peter's vision was quite vivid. As we continue the story, notice that Peter is told three times to "get up, kill and eat" all

---

[20] Injil - Acts 10:9-16

kinds of wild animals. These animals were forbidden by Jewish religious customs to eat. The vision contradicted Peter's understanding of godliness and the traditions of his culture. Therefore, Peter refused the voice in the vision three times because he didn't want to break the tradition of his fathers or violate his religious customs. Three times Peter was told, "Do not call anything impure that God has made clean." Peter understood that his vision was symbolic, but symbolic of what? He pondered the significance of the vision and waited for the meaning to unfold. It didn't take long.

> *While Peter was wondering about the meaning of the vision, the men sent by Cornelius found out where Simon's house was and stopped at the gate. They called out, asking if Simon who was known as Peter was staying there. While Peter was still thinking about the vision, the Spirit said to him, "Simon, three men are looking for you. So get up and go downstairs. Do not hesitate to go with them, for I have sent them."*
>
> *Peter went down and said to the men, "I'm the one you're looking for. Why have you come?" The men replied, "We have come from Cornelius the centurion. He is a righteous and God-fearing man, who is respected by all the Jewish people. A holy angel told him to have you come to his house so that he could hear what you have to say." Then Peter invited the men into the house to be his guests. The next day Peter started out with them, and some of the brothers from Joppa went along.*
>
> *The following day he arrived in Caesarea. Cornelius was expecting them and had called*

> *together his relatives and close friends. As Peter entered the house, Cornelius met him and fell at his feet in reverence. But Peter made him get up. "Stand up," he said, "I am only a man myself." Talking with him, Peter went inside and found a large gathering of people. He said to them: "You are well aware that it is against our law for a Jew to associate with a Gentile or visit him. But God has shown me that I should not call any man impure or unclean. So when I was sent for, I came without raising any objection. May I ask why you sent for me?"[21]*

At this point it is clear that Peter understood the meaning of his vision on the roof. He realized that God gave this vision in order to make him willing to go with the Romans who came from Cornelius. Yet Peter still did not realize the full impact of what God was about to do. Peter was still confused and wondering why Cornelius had sent for him.

> *Cornelius answered: "Four days ago I was in my house praying at this hour, at three in the afternoon. Suddenly a man in shining clothes stood before me and said, 'Cornelius, God has heard your prayer and remembered your gifts to the poor. Send to Joppa for Simon who is called Peter. He is a guest in the home of Simon the tanner, who lives by the sea.' So I sent for you immediately, and it was good of you to come. Now we are all here in the presence of God to listen to everything the Lord has commanded you to tell us."[22]*

---

[21] Injil - Acts 10:17-29
[22] Injil - Acts 10:30-33

Finally the penny dropped (he understood). God gave Peter new understanding. Peter was slowly learning that it is more important to obey God than to follow customs, if those customs prevent obedience to God. It took a powerful vision to wake Peter up and break through his prejudice. Peter gained significant insight into God's will as a result of the vision. The story continues:

> *Then Peter began to speak: "I now realize how true it is that God does not show favoritism but accepts men from every nation who fear him and do what is right. You know the message God sent to the people of Israel, telling the good news of peace through Jesus Christ, who is Lord of all. You know what has happened throughout Judea, beginning in Galilee after the baptism that John preached--how God anointed Jesus of Nazareth with the Holy Spirit and power, and how he went around doing good and healing all who were under the power of the devil, because God was with him.*
>
> *"We are witnesses of everything he did in the country of the Jews and in Jerusalem. They killed him by hanging him on a tree, but God raised him from the dead on the third day and caused him to be seen. He was not seen by all the people, but by witnesses whom God had already chosen--by us who ate and drank with him after he rose from the dead. He commanded us to preach to the people and to testify that he is the one whom God appointed as judge of the living and the dead. All the prophets testify about him that everyone who*

> *believes in him receives forgiveness of sins through his name."*
>
> *While Peter was still speaking these words, the Holy Spirit came on all who heard the message. The circumcised believers who had come with Peter were astonished that the gift of the Holy Spirit had been poured out even on the Gentiles. For they heard them speaking in tongues and praising God.*
>
> *Then Peter said, "Can anyone keep these people from being baptized with water? They have received the Holy Spirit just as we have." So he ordered that they be baptized in the name of Jesus Christ. Then they asked Peter to stay with them for a few days.*[23]

From that day the Jewish followers of Isa began to realize that the message of salvation was not just for Jews. Anyone from any nation, race, tribe or religion who trusted in Isa could be saved from the pit. The good news of Isa was good news for the whole world. A few years later, the number of non-Jewish followers of Isa far exceeded the Jewish ones. God still uses dreams and visions to point us in directions that might be contrary to certain customs and traditions in our own culture.

Interestingly, the angel in Cornelius' vision didn't tell Cornelius how to be saved. Wouldn't it have been much simpler for the angel to tell Cornelius exactly what he needed to know? Why bring Peter into the story? Couldn't the angel have done a better job than Peter (who wasn't even ready)? Why did the angel tell Cornelius to fetch Peter? The answer is quite simple. It appears that God has given the responsibility

---

[23] Injil - Acts 10:34-48

of spreading the message of salvation to followers of Isa and not to angels. Followers of Isa have been appointed by God to be the messengers of the gospel.[24] Therefore, if you want to hear the message you must talk with a follower of Isa or hear the message directly from the Injil. A dream or vision will rarely (if ever) be enough on its own. The dreamer is almost always required to take personal initiative in order to hear the rest of the story.

The angel in Cornelius' dream 'pointed' Cornelius in the right direction. We learned that it wasn't enough for Cornelius and his family to be devout and God-fearing. It wasn't enough that they did good works. Cornelius and his family needed to do something else. The same is true for us today. Being devoted and God-fearing is not enough.

---

[24] Injil - Matthew 28:18-20

Discussion Questions

1. Cornelius and Peter were God-fearing and sincere men. Is it possible to be sincere but wrong? Have you ever been sincere but wrong?

2. Why do you think the angel told Cornelius to fetch Peter rather than just tell Cornelius the message himself? Wouldn't that have been simpler?

3. Why did Peter initially refuse to obey the voice in his vision? What affect did the vision have on him?

4. What traditions, prejudices or attitudes can hinder a person from obeying God? Do any of these things hinder you from obeying God?

5. What was the message that Peter told Cornelius and his household? Can you summarize the main points?

6. How did Cornelius and his family's response to Peter's message?

7. What do these stories teach us about God's character?

Chapter 4

To Preserve His Life from Perishing (by the Sword)

A fourth reason mentioned in the scripture[25] as to why God sometimes speaks through dreams is to save people from perishing (i.e. physical death). Since we know everyone eventually dies, we understand this phrase to mean a premature death, whether by famine, storm, sickness, war, crime, etc. There are examples in the Tawrat and Injil of God sending dreams to protect people from natural disasters and violent deaths. Our first example of this type of dream comes from the Tawrat and involves the dream of a great Egyptian Pharaoh. The second example comes from the Injil and takes place after the birth of Isa.

The Dream of Pharaoh, King of Egypt: Pharaoh, King of Egypt, had two frightening dreams that none of his wise men could interpret. The cupbearer who worked in the royal palace told Pharaoh of a young Hebrew who, two years earlier, had accurately interpreted his dream and that of a companion. This young Hebrew's name was Joseph, the great grandson of Abraham. Joseph had been in an Egyptian prison for several years being punished for a crime he didn't commit. When Pharaoh learned about this young Hebrew from his cupbearer, Pharaoh immediately had Joseph called to the royal palace to interpret his dream.

---

[25] Tawrat - Job 33:14-18

So Pharaoh sent for Joseph, and he was quickly brought from the dungeon. When he had shaved and changed his clothes, he came before Pharaoh. Pharaoh said to Joseph, "I had a dream, and no one can interpret it. But I have heard it said of you that when you hear a dream you can interpret it."

"I cannot do it," Joseph replied to Pharaoh, "but God will give Pharaoh the answer he desires."

Then Pharaoh said to Joseph, "In my dream I was standing on the bank of the Nile, when out of the river there came up seven cows, fat and sleek, and they grazed among the reeds. After them, seven other cows came up--scrawny and very ugly and lean. I had never seen such ugly cows in all the land of Egypt. The lean, ugly cows ate up the seven fat cows that came up first. But even after they ate them, no one could tell that they had done so; they looked just as ugly as before. Then I woke up. "In my dreams I also saw seven heads of grain, full and good, growing on a single stalk. After them, seven other heads sprouted--withered and thin and scorched by the east wind. The thin heads of grain swallowed up the seven good heads. I told this to the magicians, but none could explain it to me." [26]

Joseph had a reputation as a master of dream interpretation, but was he? Joseph clearly declared that the interpretation of

---

[26] Tawrat - Genesis 41:14-24

> **Prophecy vs. Dream Interpretation**
> In the Tawrat and Injil, prophecy was the revelation of that which could not be known by natural means. It was revelation from God regarding the past, present or future. The interpretation of a dream from God was a type of prophecy (or supernatural revelation). Dreams from God were *not* interpreted by associating symbolic language with specific meanings like working out a formula. There is no evidence in the Tawrat, Zabur or Injil to support today's popular practice of using *dream interpretation encyclopedias or dictionaries* to decipher any cryptic language in a dream from God. The interpretation of God-sent dreams was *revealed* by God, *not* deciphered. The interpreter supernaturally understood the dreams without training in symbolic codes or dream analysis techniques. Thus the interpreter of a God-sent dream was a spokesman for God in much the same way as a prophet.

dreams belonged to God, and wasn't dependent on his personal talent or wisdom. Through supernatural revelation God made known to Joseph the true interpretation of Pharaoh's dream. Joseph then becomes a prophetic voice to Pharaoh and all of Egypt.

> *Then Joseph said to Pharaoh, "The dreams of Pharaoh are one and the same. God has revealed to Pharaoh what he is about to do. The seven good cows are seven years, and the seven good heads of grain are seven years; it is one and the same dream. The seven lean, ugly cows that came up afterward are seven years, and so are the seven worthless heads of grain scorched by the east wind: They are seven years of famine.*

> "It is just as I said to Pharaoh: God has shown Pharaoh what he is about to do. Seven years of great abundance are coming throughout the land of Egypt, but seven years of famine will follow them. Then all the abundance in Egypt will be forgotten, and the famine will ravage the land. The abundance in the land will not be remembered, because the famine that follows it will be so severe. The reason the dream was given to Pharaoh in two forms is that the matter has been firmly decided by God, and God will do it soon."[27]

God revealed to Joseph that a severe famine was going to come upon the world. And now, in keeping with his role as a prophet, God tells Joseph what Pharaoh must do to prepare for it.

> "And now let Pharaoh look for a discerning and wise man and put him in charge of the land of Egypt. Let Pharaoh appoint commissioners over the land to take a fifth of the harvest of Egypt during the seven years of abundance. They should collect all the food of these good years that are coming and store up the grain under the authority of Pharaoh, to be kept in the cities for food. This food should be held in reserve for the country, to be used during the seven years of famine that will come upon Egypt, so that the country may not be ruined by the famine."

> The plan seemed good to Pharaoh and to all his officials. So Pharaoh asked them, "Can we find

---

[27] Tawrat - Genesis 41:25-32

anyone like this man, one in whom is the spirit of God?" Then Pharaoh said to Joseph, "Since God has made all this known to you, there is no one so discerning and wise as you. You shall be in charge of my palace, and all my people are to submit to your orders. Only with respect to the throne will I be greater than you." So Pharaoh said to Joseph, "I hereby put you in charge of the whole land of Egypt." Then Pharaoh took his signet ring from his finger and put it on Joseph's finger. He dressed him in robes of fine linen and put a gold chain around his neck. He had him ride in a chariot as his second-in-command, and men shouted before him, "Make way!" Thus he put him in charge of the whole land of Egypt.[28]

God sent the dream to Pharaoh because he didn't want everyone in the land to starve to death. The dream was a demonstration of God's love. By telling Pharaoh what was going to happen Pharaoh could prepare for the day of disaster and no one would have to die.

In contrast to King Nebuchadnezzar of Babylon (see Chapter 2), the Egyptian Pharaoh listened carefully to the interpretation (or prophecy) of his dreams and acted upon it. Many lives were saved not only in Egypt but also in the surrounding nations who came and purchased food from the Egyptians' surplus. Because God is merciful and kind he gives dreams to save people from premature death.

The Dreams of Joseph (Stepfather of Isa):
The following dreams also involve a man named Joseph, but a different Joseph from our previous story. Their lives are

---

[28] Tawrat – Genesis 41:33-43

separated by nearly 2,000 years. This story is from the Injil and focuses on the events immediately after the birth of Isa. These are the dreams of Joseph, a descendent of David and the stepfather of Isa. Joseph was a righteous man who made his living as a carpenter. This story takes place while Isa was still a young child.

Isa was born in Palestine during a very dangerous time. The country was under the rule of a ruthless king named Herod the Great (37–4 BC). He wasn't called Herod the Great because he did great things but because he was the first of several Palestinian kings in named Herod. History tells us that Herod was a half Jew, appointed to his position by the Senate in Rome. He was considered cruel even by the standards of his day. He murdered all his political opponents and anyone who he considered a threat to his rule, including his wife, three sons and numerous relatives. The Roman Emperor Augustus was prompted to ridicule him by saying, "It is better to be Herod's pig than to be his son." Even on his deathbed Herod was cruel. Only a few days from death, he commanded all the principal men of the Jewish nation to come to his presence. Whereupon Herod had them immediately locked up in the hippodrome and surrounded them with soldiers, ordering that immediately after his own death, they should be killed, so there would be honorable "mourning" at his funeral. King Herod the Great was a wicked, violent and dreadful tyrant.

A bust of Herod the "Great"

The story of Isa's birth took place during the reign of Herod the Great. It describes how King Herod plotted to have Isa killed while he was still a child. As you will see, the dreams in this story did not need any interpretation. Each person who received a dream knew exactly what the dream meant and what to do.

> *After Jesus was born in Bethlehem in Judea, during the time of King Herod, Magi[29] from the east came to Jerusalem and asked, "Where is the one who has been born king of the Jews? We saw his star in the east and have come to worship him."*
>
> *When King Herod heard this he was disturbed, and all Jerusalem with him. When he had called together all the people's chief priests and teachers of the law, he asked them where the Christ was to be born. "In Bethlehem in Judea," they replied, "for this is what the prophet has written:*
>
>> *'But you, Bethlehem, in the land of Judah, are by no means least among the rulers of Judah; for out of you will come a ruler who will be the shepherd of my people Israel.'*
>
> *Then Herod called the Magi secretly and found out from them the exact time the star had appeared. He sent them to Bethlehem and said, "Go and make a careful search for the child. As*

---

[29] Magi were non-Jewish astrologers or wise men probably from Persia or Arabia.

soon as you find him, report to me, so that I too may go and worship him."

After they had heard the king, they went on their way, and the star they had seen in the east went ahead of them until it stopped over the place where the child was. When they saw the star, they were overjoyed. On coming to the house, they saw the child with his mother Mary, and they bowed down and worshiped him. Then they opened their treasures and presented him with gifts of gold and of incense and of myrrh. And having been warned in a dream not to go back to Herod, they returned to their country by another route.

When they had gone, an angel of the Lord appeared to Joseph in a dream. "Get up," he said, "take the child and his mother and escape to Egypt. Stay there until I tell you, for Herod is going to search for the child to kill him." So he got up, took the child and his mother during the night and left for Egypt, where he stayed until the death of Herod. And so was fulfilled what the Lord had said through the prophet: "Out of Egypt I called my son." When Herod realized that he had been outwitted by the Magi, he was furious, and he gave orders to kill all the boys in Bethlehem and its vicinity who were two years old and under, in accordance with the time he had learned from the Magi.

Then what was said through the prophet Jeremiah was fulfilled: "A voice is heard in Ramah, weeping and great mourning, Rachel *weeping for her children and refusing to be comforted, because they are no more."*

After Herod died, an angel of the Lord appeared in a dream to Joseph in Egypt and said, "Get up, take the child and his mother and go to the land of Israel, for those who were trying to take the child's life are dead." So he got up, took the child and his mother and went to the land of Israel. But when he heard that Archelaus was reigning in Judea in place of his father Herod, he was afraid to go there. Having been warned in a dream, he withdrew to the district of Galilee, and he went and lived in a town called Nazareth."[30]

In this story we find several examples of God using dreams to protect people from death. First, God warned the Magi in a dream. Magi were wise men from the east, probably from Arabia or Persia (ancient Babylon). They had understood from studying ancient prophecy and astronomy that a great king of the Jews was to be born. They wanted to honor him with gifts. After they found Isa, God warned them in a dream not to return to King Herod. The Magi were obedient to the warning and outwitted Herod and returned to their own country by another route.

In this story God sent an angel to speak to Joseph in a dream who told him to immediately flee to Egypt in order to save the young Isa's life. The very night Joseph received the dream he obeyed. He left everything they had and traveled to a foreign land. After living in Egypt for a few years Joseph had another dream where he was told to take his family back to Israel. Again, Joseph was quick to obey.

---

[30] Injil - Matthew 2:1-18

For reasons known only to God, it seems that some events in life are fixed and unchangeable—even events that bring suffering, death and destruction (i.e. a famine or rule of an evil dictator). Instead of changing the event, God demonstrates his love by warning people so they can avoid the full consequences of the event. God wants us to act on any revelation he gives us. In both stories of this chapter we see that obedient action was required in order to benefit from the warning of the dreams.

Discussion Questions

1. Why weren't Pharaoh's magicians able to interpret Pharaoh's dreams? Certainly their collective knowledge about dreams was greater than that of the young Hebrew Joseph.

2. God sent dreams to warn Pharaoh of the famine instead of preventing the famine from happening in the first place. Any ideas why?

3. Did Pharaoh's dreams save lives or was it Pharaoh's response to his dreams that saved lives? Explain.

4. Why did King Herod want to destroy Isa?

5. Who received dreams of warning concerning the King Herod? What were these warnings?

6. What do these stories teach us about God? What questions do they raise?

Chapter 5

How Can You Tell if a Dream is from God?

This is an important question. Having a dream from God is a serious thing and shouldn't be treated lightly. But as we all know, just because a person "thinks" he had a dream from God doesn't make it so. Many people in the past have provoked the Lord to anger by falsely assuming they had a dream from God. It says in the Tawrat:

> *"Yes," declares the LORD, "I am against the prophets who wag their own tongues and yet declare, 'The LORD declares.' Indeed, I am against those who prophesy false dreams," declares the LORD. "They tell them and lead my people astray with their reckless lies, yet I did not send or appoint them. They do not benefit these people in the least," declares the LORD.*[31]

God is against those who lead people astray by the reckless lies of false dreams. Therefore we need to be very careful to test a dream before we accept it as a dream from God. The Injil gives the following advice regarding prophecy and the advice is also valid for dreams.

> *Do not treat prophecies with contempt. Test everything. Hold on to the good. Avoid every kind of evil.*[32]

---

[31] Tawrat - Jeremiah 23:30
[32] Injil - 1 Thessalonians 5:20-22

We are not to treat prophecies (or dreams from God) with contempt but are to test everything. But how do we test dreams? We would like to suggest five guidelines. While these guidelines are not necessarily comprehensive, they provide a good starting point to help you test if a dream is from God or not.

Guidelines for Testing Dreams:
1. Understand that all dreams are not from God.
2. Confirm that the dream doesn't conflict with the Scriptures.
3. Consult with followers of Isa about the dream.
4. Discern the purpose and character of the dream.
5. Nurture a willingness to obey God.

1. Understand that all dreams are not from God
The Scriptures teach that God is not the source behind every extraordinary dream. One step in testing if a dream is from God is to reduce the possibility that the dream has another source. For example, you should know that most dreams are a result of our normal sleep cycle (see box on following page). The source of many extraordinary dreams can be traced to things that affect our mind. Anything that can affect our mind can affect our dreams. For example, memories, anxiety, fear, attitudes, expectations, and chemicals (such as alcohol and drugs) are just a few. The concept of "mind" in the Tawrat and Injil is often coupled with the words heart, soul and spirit. It is a term that includes more than just our brain or "thinking." It refers to the whole inner life of man's subjective experiences of thinking, knowing, feeling, willing, etc. When we use the term "mind" in this chapter we use it in the same sense.

Over the years many people have been deceived by dreams that they falsely thought came from God. The Tawrat warns us that even some who claim to be prophets can have false dreams.

"I have heard what the prophets say who prophesy lies in my name. They say, 'I had a dream! I had a dream!' How long will this continue in the hearts of these lying prophets, who prophesy the delusions of their own minds?" [33]

From the passage above it is clear that some dreams come from the delusions of the human mind. By definition, a delusion is something fake or false that is believed to be genuine or true. Since the human mind is susceptible to delusions, we must be slow to assume that a dream is from God. Before we can judge if an extraordinary dream is from God we should rule out the possibility that the dream was caused by something else. For example, can the source of the

---

Facts About the Normal Sleep Cycle: Most dreams are a natural function of the human mind while sleeping. A lot of useful clinical research has been done on sleep and dreams over the past 60 years. In 1953 continuous monitoring of electromagnetic brain activity led to the discovery of 3-4 different stages of sleep. The deepest stage of sleep is called Rapid Eye Movement (REM) sleep. During REM sleep the brain is very active, the eyes move back and forth rapidly under the lids, and the large muscles of the body are relaxed.

Research shows that our most vivid dreams occur during REM sleep. This classic research demonstrated that REM sleep occurs every 90-100 minutes, three to four times at night, and lasts longer as the night progresses. We dream on average at least one or two hours every night and often have four to seven dreams in one night. Even when we sleep our minds do not shut down or rest. On the contrary, during REM sleep our mind is very active even though all our major body muscles are completely relaxed.

---

[33] Tawrat - Jeremiah 23:23

dream be traced to emotional anxiety, chemical imbalances, or even evil spirits? All of these are known sources of delusion.

a. Anxiety

Mental or emotional anxiety is a common source of extraordinary dreams. When our mind is troubled it will often be reflected by vivid dreams or nightmares. Nightmares and disturbing dreams are a sign of anxiety. Many things may cause this turmoil, including fear, trauma, bitterness, pain, illness, allergies, etc. There is a proverb recorded in the Zabur that says:

> *As a dream comes when there are many*
> *cares, so the speech of a fool when there are*
> *many words.*[34]

In this proverb the Zabur affirms a common experience of man (i.e. worry and fear effects our dream life). Traumatic events like divorce, sickness, accidents, grief, violence, etc. can produce emotional stress and nightmares. These are called Post-traumatic stress nightmares (PSN) and are

---

Clinical research has revealed that if a person is woken during their REM sleep they can remember the details of their dream better than if they wake up naturally. On average, five minutes after the end of the dream, half the content is forgotten. After ten minutes 90% is lost. About one third of our lives are spent sleeping. By the time you are thirty years old you will have spent over 87,600 hours (3,650 days) or nearly ten years sleeping and at least three years of that dreaming.

Note: The Tawrat, Zabur and Injil never ask or encourage us to seek meaning from our dreams even though we spend up to 10% of our lives dreaming!

---

[34] Zabur - Ecclesiastes 5:3

common among trauma survivors. Even seemingly harmless "trauma" like a late night horror movie on TV can traumatize both adults and children causing PSN nightmares for months. In the same way, bitterness, anger, resentment, and jealousy can also cause nightmares or disturbing dreams. Our state of mind (emotions, will, feelings, thoughts, etc.) plays a key role in how we dream. Dreams birthed from mental or emotional anxiety may be revealing but are part of the inner complexities of the human mind and are not in the same category as dreams from God. When God gives a dream to an anxious person, other characteristics of the dream will provide evidence that the dream was from God and not just stemming from the anxiety itself.

b. Chemical Imbalance
Alcohol and drugs are often the cause of hallucinations and vivid dreams. Similarly malnutrition, sleep deprivation, dizziness, and indigestion can cause chemical imbalances and mental distortions that can influence dreams. Narcotics and alcohol are infamous for altering the state of our mind and producing hallucinations (i.e. false visions). Even the Zabur acknowledges the hallucinating and delusional affects of alcohol on the mind.

> *Do not gaze at wine when it is red, when it sparkles in the cup, when it goes down smoothly! In the end it bites like a snake and poisons like a viper. Your eyes will see strange sights and your mind imagine confusing things.*[35]

Some people use alcohol or other drugs to enhance dreams and hallucinations for so-called "religious" experiences.

---

[35] Zabur – Proverbs 23:31-33

However the dreams and visions produced by such practices are not from God but from the delusions of the mind.

c. Evil Spirits (jinn)

Evil spirits can also be the cause of extraordinary dreams and visions.[36] Many Hindus and New Age enthusiasts are among those who view dreaming as an important means of communicating with spirits and "divine" powers. According to this worldview, spirits can be good, bad or neutral. Mediums and spiritists are people who attempt to contact the spiritual realm to seek supernatural guidance or special favors for themselves or their clients. Typically, they do this through dreams, trances, séances, or any number of rituals. Much of the literature written about dreams and the interpretation of dreams comes from people with a worldview that is radically different from the worldview presented in the Tawrat, Zabur and Injil.

The Tawrat acknowledges that it is possible for humans to make contact with the spirit world. However, the Tawrat is very clear that communicating with spirits is detestable in God's eyes. In the Tawrat and Injil humans are commanded to pray to God alone and not to angels, demons or the spirits of the dead. Making contact with spirits will lead to further confusion and deception. Concerning mediums, spiritists and those who communicate with spirits the Tawrat says:

> *Let no one be found among you who ... practices divination or sorcery, interprets*

---

[36] In the Injil (Matthew 4:1-10) Satan tempted Isa by taking him to a very high mountain and showing him all the kingdoms of the world and their splendor. Since we know of no actual mountain from where all the kingdoms of the world can be physically seen, it is most probable that Isa was shown all the kingdoms of the world in a vision. If so, this is a specific example from the Injil demonstrating that the evil spirits can influence visions (and thus dreams as well).

omens, engages in witchcraft, or casts spells, or who is a medium or spiritist or who consults the dead. Anyone who does these things is detestable to the LORD...[37]

"Do not turn to mediums or seek out spiritists, for you will be defiled by them. I am the LORD your God."[38]

In the Tawrat and Injil, angels (good spirits) don't communicate with human beings unless God sends them. The Tawrat and Injil teach us to pray to and worship God alone. We are forbidden to seek the counsel of spirits, not even angels. Angels are obedient to God and therefore do not communicate with humans unless commanded to do so by God.

The same cannot be said about evil spirits (demons or jinn). Demons both initiate contact with humans and answer people who seek to contact spirits. If you try to contact spirits through dreams, mediums or spiritists you can be sure that only evil spirits will be on hand to answer you. Seeking guidance from spirits or any attempt to contact spirits will open doors to evil spirits that may be difficult to close. *God has not ordained spirits to give guidance to humans. God has reserved that role for himself.* In the Injil, followers of Isa were cautioned about being deceived by spirits. The Injil says that even Satan disguises himself to appear like an angel.

... for Satan himself masquerades as an angel of light.[39]

---

[37] Tawrat - Deuteronomy 18:13
[38] Tawrat - Leviticus 19:31
[39] Injil - 2 Corinthians 11:14

Therefore, if you attempt to use dreams as a way of contacting the spirit world you are acting as a medium and spiritist and thus disobeying God. If you contact a spirit you can be sure that it is a demon (perhaps masquerading as good spirit). You are on a road that will lead to nightmares, more fear, and spiritual bondage.

2. Confirm that the dream does not conflict with the Tawrat, Zabur or Injil

Another step in testing if a dream is from God is confirming that the dream doesn't conflict with the teachings of the Tawrat, Zabur or Injil. God's word is more reliable and certain than any dream. God will not contradict in a dream the guidance he has already given in the Scriptures. You can be certain that any dream from God will not refute, invalidate or "update" the teachings of the Tawrat, Zabur and Injil. The better you know these holy books, the better prepared you will be to understand if a dream is from God or not. It is written:

> *"Let the prophet who has a dream tell his dream, but let the one who has my word speak it faithfully. For what has straw to do with grain?" declares the LORD. "Is not my word like fire," declares the LORD, "and like a hammer that breaks a rock in pieces?"* [40]

In the passage above, God's word is said to be as superior to dreams as grain is superior to straw. Scripture is the "bench mark" by which we test the validity of God-given dreams. We can be completely certain that dreams from God will never promote murder, deception, sexual immorality, lying, theft, greed, selfishness or false doctrine. For example, we heard the story of a man who claimed God clearly told him in a dream to leave his wife and children and move in with a younger

---

[40] Tawrat - Jeremiah 23:28-29

woman he had recently met. This dream was not from God but a delusion of his own mind. Dreams from God will never promote or encourage anything that is contrary to what God has already revealed in the Tawrat, Zabur and Injil.

A thorough knowledge of the Scriptures can be essential in discerning if an extraordinary dream is from God. Therefore it is strongly recommended that you consult with a knowledgeable follower of Isa who has a good understanding of the Tawrat, Zabur and Injil.

3. Consult with followers of Isa about the dream
In chapter 3 we read how devout people were directed to seek out followers of Isa in their dreams. Cornelius the Roman captain and Saul the persecutor were devout and earnest men who wanted to please God. As devout as they were, they still lacked key information in their knowledge of God. Peter came and explained to Cornelius the message of Isa and Ananias came to Saul and prayed for his healing. God sent followers of Isa to both of these devout men. God gave both men a vision but used followers of Isa to explain the meaning and purpose of their visions.

Not every follower of Isa has a gift of prophecy or an ability to supernaturally interpret dreams, but some do. It may be more common to find a follower of Isa that has a good understanding of the Tawrat, Zabur and Injil. If they don't, they should know someone who does and put you in touch with him or her.

We saw from the previous chapters that dreams from God were interpreted by God's people. Both the Pharaoh of Egypt and King Nebuchadnezzar needed interpreters to understand their dreams. Their own astrologers, wise men and sorcerers were not enough to interpret dreams from God. Modern day astrologers, wise men or spiritualists may be able to interpret dreams that are influenced by anxiety or evil spirits, *but not dreams from the one true God.*

Today God regularly uses followers of Isa to help people understand the meaning of dreams from God. The purpose of the dreams is often quite clear and free from riddles and symbolic language.

4. Discern the purpose of the dream
In chapters 1 through 4 we identified four reasons God gives dreams. These were to: 1) Turn people from wrongdoing; 2) Keep them from pride; 3) Preserve souls from the pit and 4) Protect them from perishing by the sword. While God never promised to limit his dreams to these four categories,[41] they provide four common characteristics of God-given dreams. *If your dream fits into at least one of these categories, it shares a known characteristic of God-given dreams.*

From our interviews and research, "pointing dreams" or dreams to "preserve souls from the pit" were very common. There were examples of all four types of dreams as well as a few dreams that didn't fit neatly into any of the categories. Most were very simple and many needed no interpretation. The meaning of many dreams became clear after talking with a follower of Isa or by reading the Injil. Some dreams had similar themes. For example:

---

[41] There is a fifth category of dreams and visions found in the Tawrat and Injil not discussed in this booklet. Those are the dreams God gave the prophets. It is written in the Tawrat, *"When a prophet of the Lord is among you, I reveal myself to him in visions, I speak to him in dreams" (Numbers 12:6).* The prophets often received their messages through dreams or visions and many of these are recorded in the Tawrat. See Isaiah 1:1; Ezekiel 1:1; Daniel; Hosea 12:10. This book was written to help you understand and respond to your dream, a dream that would not be in this fifth category.

In one woman's dream, *a bright shinning figure (whom she instinctively understood to be Isa) appeared to her and gave her a white wedding dress to put on. She tried to fit the dress over what she was wearing but realized that the new dress would not fit unless she took off the old one.* Prior to this dream, it had not crossed the woman's mind to read about the life of Isa. Now, however, the woman was so curious that she found an Injil and began to read it. She realized the meaning of her dream as she read the Injil.

In another woman's dream, *God was holding a wonderful gift of light that he wanted to give to her. In her dream she continually refused the gift, opting to hold on to the things she already had. After she woke up she bitterly regretted that she refused the gift.* Later that same week she met a follower of Isa for the first time and learned that Isa said:

> *I am the light of the world. Whoever follows me will never walk in darkness, but will have the light of life.*[42]

Upon hearing this, the woman immediately remembered her dream and realized that the gift of light in her dream was Isa.

Throughout history true followers of Isa have been persecuted and mistreated no matter where they live. Interestingly, the people to whom God gives dreams often come from families and/or societies where following Isa is not socially acceptable. These people would never have considered following Isa if it weren't for their dreams. Their dreams caught their attention and created a desire to hear more about Isa. Often the purpose of a God-given dream is simply to encourage a person to learn more about the life and teachings of Isa.

---

[42] Injil - John 8:12

5. Nurture a willingness to obey God

Dreams from God normally require some action or response from the dreamer. Such was the case in the dreams we read about in the Tawrat and Injil. Action was expected of the dreamer in order to benefit from the dream. Willingness to obey is normally a prerequisite to understanding God's will. We cannot expect to know God's will (like the meaning of a dream from God) unless we are willing to act in obedience. Isa put it this way:

> *If anyone chooses to do God's will, he will find out whether my teaching comes from God or whether I speak on my own.*[43]

Notice that choosing "to do God's will" is a prerequisite for understanding. God is not predisposed to reveal the mysteries of his will to those who are unwilling to do it. Sometimes, however, God gives dreams even to stubborn people (like King Nebuchadnezzar). He does this in order to give them a chance to humble themselves and obey. Without a willingness to obey God, there is no profit or purpose in understanding dreams from him.

One of the saddest things we have seen is people who do nothing about their dream. They ignore it or don't know what step to take in order to understand. God rarely forces us to do anything and he will not force you to listen to your dream.

Another woman had a dream, *and in her dream two young women came to her door to share with her the 'word of life.' She didn't know what was meant by the term 'word of life' in her dream.* Soon afterwards two young women did come to

---

[43] Injil - John 7:17

her door and started speaking with her about Isa. She learned that Isa is called the 'Word of life'[44] in the Injil.

Sadly, 13 years have passed and this woman still has not responded to God's message. She is frightened by what her neighbors and relatives might think if she obeys the message she heard. We are afraid of what will happen to her soul if she doesn't obey. A few months ago, a friend had several dreams about Isa. Although he can still remember his dreams as clearly as if they happened yesterday, he ignores them because he knows that if he responds his life will change. His fear makes him blind and passive. It reminds me of how, when Isa entered the city of Jerusalem 2,000 years ago, the people there rejected the message he had for them. He said:

> *If you, even you, had only known on this day what would bring you peace--but now it is hidden from your eyes. The days will come upon you when your enemies will build an embankment against you and encircle you... because you did not recognize the time of God's coming to you.*[45]

He prophesied that disastrous consequences awaited those who remain blind as passive to God's message. Some people wonder why God doesn't speak to them. They say, "If only God would speak to me or show me a miracle, then I'd get more serious." Unfortunately, just as in Isa's day, the problem isn't that God is silent. The problem is that very few people are listening. God reveals himself to human beings in both general and specific ways. God reveals himself in a general way through his creation. It says in the Injil:

---

[44] Injil - 1 John 1:1
[45] Injil - Luke 19:42-44

For since the creation of the world God's invisible qualities--his eternal power and divine nature--have been clearly seen, being understood from what has been made, so that men are without excuse.[46]

Maybe in your dream God was speaking to you, but unless you have an interest in hearing from God you may not bother to listen to his voice. The Roman Captain Cornelius needed to act upon the message he received in his vision. He sent for Peter immediately even though he didn't know who Peter was or what he would say. And because Cornelius was determined to hear what God had to say to him, God was pleased to bless Cornelius and his family. Isa illustrated just how valuable God's message is:

"... the kingdom of heaven is like a merchant looking for fine pearls. When he found one of great value, he went away and sold everything he had and bought it."[47]

Seeking after God is worth whatever it costs you. Having a dream or vision about Isa can be both the worst and the best thing to happen to you. It can be the worst thing if you ignore or reject what God is saying to you. By ignoring his words you move farther away from God. Or it can be the best thing to happen to you, if you act on your dream and seek God. Isa promised:

"Ask and it will be given to you; seek and you will find; knock and the door will be opened to you. For everyone who asks receives; he who

---

[46] Injil - Romans 1:20
[47] Injil - Matthew 13:45-46

seeks finds; and to him who knocks, the door will be opened."[48]

I have come that they may have life, and have it to the full. "I am the good shepherd. The good shepherd lays down his life for the sheep."[49]

One thing is clear; you need to actively pursue what God is saying to you. This is the topic of the next chapter, "Responding to God's Revelation."

---

[48] Injil - Matthew 7:7-11
[49] Injil - John 10:10

Discussion Questions

1. What are the most common sources of dreams?

2. Why must we be very careful before we claim a dream is from God?

3. Which of the five guidelines in this chapter do you think is the most difficult to understand or apply?

4. Why would God conceal the meaning of a dream?

5. Are you willing to obey God even if it means:
   a. Forgiving your enemies
   b. Losing face
   c. Becoming poor
   d. Being persecuted and mistreated
   e. Reconciling with those you have wronged
   f. All of the above

6. Have you ever had a dream that you think is from God? What was it?

Chapter 6

Responding to God's Revelation

In the Tawrat, Zabur and Injil we discover a God who is interested and involved with his creation. Isa was moved to say:

> *Are not two sparrows sold for a penny? Yet not one of them will fall to the ground apart from the will of your Father (God). And even the very hairs of your head are all numbered. So don't be afraid; you are worth more than many sparrows.*[50]

Peter, one of Isa disciples, also understood how much God values people. He wrote:

> *Cast all your anxiety on him (God) because he cares for you.*[51]

If God has given you a dream it is probably because he wants to catch your attention so you will know that he loves and cares about you. However, as great as dreams are, God has given us revelation that is far more reliable and certain than dreams. As important as the Tawrat, Zabur and Injil are, they are not God's greatest revelation to humanity. God's greatest revelation to humanity is not a dream nor a book, but a person.

God's Greatest Revelation: In the Tawrat, Zabur and Injil we find revelations about God and his dealings with humanity. One of the main surprises is that God's message was not sent

---

[50] Injil - Matt 10:29-31
[51] Injil - 1 Peter 5:7

down from heaven in the form of a book, but in the form of a person. The Injil expresses it like this:

> *In the beginning was the Word, and the Word was with God, and the Word was God. He was with God in the beginning. Through him all things were made; without him nothing was made that has been made. In him was life, and that life was the light of men. The light shines in the darkness, but the darkness has not understood it.* [52]

We learn that the *Word* was with God, in fact, that the *Word* was God. But what does it mean when it says *Word?* To understand we need to read on:

> *The Word became flesh and made his dwelling among us. We have seen his glory, the glory of the One and Only, who came from the Father, full of grace and truth.* [53]

The Injil is making the extraordinary claim that God's Word actually came and lived among us on earth. Furthermore, it claims that Isa is the "Word." The point is that Isa is more than a prophet or great messenger of God. *Isa is God's message and greatest revelation.* Isa made some surprising statements about who he was, and especially how he himself was the answer to humanity's greatest needs. Let's take a look at some of them.

Isa's Claims about Himself: Many philosophers through the ages have agreed that there is a deep hunger in the human heart. In the last century, the famous philosopher-

---

[52] Injil - John 1:1-4
[53] Injil - John 1:14

psychologist Sigmund Freud believed people were hungry for love. Another, named Carl Jung, maintained people were hungry for security. A third, named Alfred Adler, concluded people were hungry for significance. In contrast, Isa said, *"I am the Bread of Life."* In other words, if you want to satisfy your inner hungers, Isa says, "Come to me."

> *Then Jesus declared, "I am the bread of life. He who comes to me will never go hungry, and he who believes in me will never be thirsty."*[54]

Many people feel like they are walking in darkness, disillusionment and despair. They don't know where to turn and are looking for direction. Isa said to such people:

> *"I am the light of the world. Whoever follows me will never walk in darkness, but will have the light of life."*[55]

Many are fearful of death. Fear of death is something that has been with mankind since the beginning. However, Isa made this staggering claim about himself:

> *"I am the resurrection and the life. He who believes in me will live, even though he dies; and whoever lives and believes in me will never die."*[56]

People from all backgrounds and nations, rich and poor are burdened by worries, anxieties, fears, and guilt. People are burdened with the weight of keeping religious laws and

---

[54] Injil - John 6:35
[55] Injil - John 8:12
[56] Injil - John 11:25-26

traditions that don't satisfy their thirst for God. Isa says to them:

> *"Come to me, all you who are weary and burdened, and I will give you rest. Take my yoke upon you and learn from me, for I am gentle and humble in heart, and you will find rest for your souls. For my yoke is easy and my burden is light."*[57]

Many people are looking for truth. Faced with different religions, philosophies and ideas they are confused and don't know what is true or how to find God. Isa says to them:

> *"I am the way and the truth and the life. No one comes to the Father except through me."*[58]

The list of extraordinary claims Isa made about himself goes on. For example, on one occasion he encountered a man who was paralyzed.

> *A few days later, when Jesus again entered Capernaum, the people heard that he had come home. So many gathered that there was no room left, not even outside the door, and he preached the word to them. Some men came, bringing to him a paralytic, carried by four of them. Since they could not get him to Jesus because of the crowd, they made an opening in the roof above Jesus and, after digging through it, lowered the mat the paralyzed man was lying on. When Jesus saw their faith, he said to the paralytic, "Son, your sins are forgiven."*

---

[57] Injil - Matthew 11:28-30
[58] Injil - John 14:6

> *Now some teachers of the law were sitting there, thinking to themselves, "Why does this fellow talk like that? He's blaspheming! Who can forgive sins but God alone?" Immediately Jesus knew in his spirit that this was what they were thinking in their hearts, and he said to them, "Why are you thinking these things? Which is easier: to say to the paralytic, 'Your sins are forgiven,' or to say, 'Get up, take your mat and walk'? But that you may know that the Son of Man has authority on earth to forgive sins . . ." He said to the paralytic, "I tell you, get up, take your mat and go home." He got up, took his mat and walked out in full view of them all. This amazed everyone and they praised God, saying, "We have never seen anything like this!"* [59]

The reaction of the religious leaders was, *"Why does he talk like that? He's blaspheming! Who can forgive sins but God alone?"* Isa went on to prove his authority to forgive sins by healing the paralyzed man. This claim to be able to forgive sins was indeed astonishing.

Another claim Isa made about himself was that one day he would judge the world. He said that on that day all the nations would be gathered before him and he would pass judgment on them. Some would inherit eternal life and others would suffer the punishment of being separated from God forever.

> *"When the Son of Man comes in his glory, and all the angels with him, he will sit on his throne in heavenly glory. All the nations will be*

---

[59] Injil - Mark 2:1-12

> *gathered before him, and he will separate the people one from another as a shepherd separates the sheep from the goats."* [60]

But here is where his claim becomes even more startling, because he added that not only would he be the judge; he will also be the criterion of judgment. In other words, what happens to us on the Day of Judgment depends on how we respond to Isa in this life!

> *He will put the sheep on his right and the goats on his left. "Then the King will say to those on his right, 'Come, you who are blessed by my Father; take your inheritance, the kingdom prepared for you since the creation of the world. For I was hungry and you gave me something to eat, I was thirsty and you gave me something to drink, I was a stranger and you invited me in, I needed clothes and you clothed me, I was sick and you looked after me, I was in prison and you came to visit me.' Then the righteous will answer him, 'Lord, when did we see you hungry and feed you, or thirsty and give you something to drink? When did we see you a stranger and invite you in, or needing clothes and clothe you? When did we see you sick or in prison and go to visit you?' The King will reply, 'I tell you the truth, whatever you did for one of the least of these brothers of mine, you did for me.'*
>
> *"Then he will say to those on his left, 'Depart from me, you who are cursed, into the eternal fire prepared for the devil and his angels. For I*

---

[60] Injil - Matt 25:31-32

> *was hungry and you gave me nothing to eat, I was thirsty and you gave me nothing to drink, I was a stranger and you did not invite me in, I needed clothes and you did not clothe me, I was sick and in prison and you did not look after me.' They also will answer, 'Lord, when did we see you hungry or thirsty or a stranger or needing clothes or sick or in prison, and did not help you?' He will reply, 'I tell you the truth, whatever you did not do for one of the least of these, you did not do for me.' Then they will go away to eternal punishment, but the righteous to eternal life."* [61]

On another occasion we find Isa talking to his disciples. Even though he had spent much time with them, they were still confused as to exactly who he was. What he told them was this:

> *"Anyone who has seen me has seen the Father (God). How can you say, 'Show us the Father'? Don't you believe that I am in the Father, and that the Father is in me? The words I say to you are not just my own. Rather, it is the Father, living in me, who is doing his work. Believe me when I say that I am in the Father and the Father is in me; or at least believe on the evidence of the miracles themselves."* [62]

Isa was saying 'if you want to know what God is like then look at me. If you want to know what God's message for humanity is then listen to my words.' No disrespect intended, but we must make a choice. If Isa was not who he said he

---

[61] Injil - Matt 25:33-46
[62] Injil - John 14:9-11

was, then he must be either a liar or a madman, or both. What else is there to conclude? Anyone can make great claims about themselves, and indeed many have, but there is overwhelming evidence to support Isa's claims. Let's take a brief look at his life and death to find out if the things he did support his claim to be the *Word* of God.

Isa's Miracles: Isa said that the miracles he performed were evidence that God was with him, and indeed some of the miracles he performed had never been seen before. He went to a party and turned water into wine.[63] He had control over the weather so one day when he was in a boat in a storm he rebuked the wind and the waves. They obeyed him.[64] He did some remarkable healings: opening the eyes of people born blind, causing the deaf and dumb to hear and speak, and enabling cripples to walk.[65] He set many people free from evil spirits that controlled their lives, and on three occasions he raised dead people back to life. These are just a few of the great miracles he did which backed up his claims about who he was.

Isa's Character: When you think of great religious leaders, maybe you think of people who were aloof and unapproachable. Not so with Isa. As we read the account of his life in the Injil, we find people loved to be in his company. The extraordinary thing was the kind of people who loved to be in Isa's company. It was the untouchables and marginalized people of his day; the prostitutes, the lepers, the poor, and the working class. In other words, those considered lowly in society. It is significant to keep in mind that these people were impressed, not so much by Isa's miracles, but by his love for them. Despite their sins, Isa loved and cared for

---

[63] Injil - John 2:1-11
[64] Injil - Mark 5:35-41
[65] Injil - John 5:1-9

them. In fact, it was love that motivated all the miracles he performed.

Even his death testified to the strength of his character and love. When enemies had Isa arrested, one of his disciples was ready to defend him with a sword. He was ready to fight and defend him. But listen to what Isa told them:

> *"Put your sword back in its place," Jesus said to him, "for all who draw the sword will die by the sword. Do you think I cannot call on my Father, and he will at once put at my disposal more than twelve legions of angels? But how then would the Scriptures be fulfilled that say it must happen in this way?"*[66]

Isa was not defenseless. He could have called down help from heaven and been rescued. Yet Isa had the strength of character to restrain his power so the prophecy about him could be fulfilled. He had to be executed on the cross in order to pay the penalty of our sin. He loved us and gave his life in exchange for ours. Even when his enemies had captured, tortured and nailed him to a cross, he demonstrated his love again by praying:

> *"Father, forgive them for they do not know what they're doing."* [67]

Are these the characteristics of a liar or madman, or are these the characteristics of a person you would be willing to live and die for?

---

[66] Injil - Matthew 26:54
[67] Injil - Luke 22:34

Isa's Resurrection: After Isa was crucified and died, his body was laid in a tomb. But on the third day, when some of his followers came to put spices on the body (a custom of the day), they had the shock of their lives when they discovered his body was missing. Angels appeared to these followers and told them that God had raised Isa from the dead! Later Isa appeared to his followers and reassured them. There were more than 500 eyewitnesses to his resurrection from the dead before he was taken up into heaven.[68]

Throughout history many men have been great teachers. A few have done great miracles. But none have ever risen from the dead. God's raising Isa from the dead is the greatest validation of his amazing claims about himself. No one but God could have raised Isa from the dead. God's greatest revelation to us is not a book or a dream but a person. God's greatest revelation is Isa, also known as Jesus Christ!

Taking a Step of Faith: What about you? Isa wants to save your soul from the pit and rescue you from eternal death. He wants to free you from spiritual bondage and make you fully alive. Isa invites you to be his follower and little brother, but he won't force you. Love must be freely given and freely accepted. But if you reject Isa's invitation to believe and follow him you will suffer the consequences. You will be compelled to continue in your own sin and shame away from the presence of God both now and forever. But if you believe in Isa your honor will be restored and God will call you his child and friend. You will become born again to a new life of love and spiritual freedom. One thing is certain: you cannot listen and do nothing. The choice is yours. The Injil says:

> *For God so loved the world that he gave his one and only Son, that whoever believes in him*

---

[68] Injil - Matthew chapters 27-28 and John chapters 18-21

shall not perish but have eternal life. For God did not send his Son into the world to condemn the world, but to save the world through him. Whoever believes in him is not condemned, but whoever does not believe stands condemned already because he has not believed in the name of God's one and only Son. This is the verdict: Light has come into the world, but men loved darkness instead of light because their deeds were evil.[69]

I tell you the truth, whoever hears my word and believes him who sent me has eternal life and will not be condemned; he has crossed over from death to life.[70]

"The time has come," Jesus said. "The kingdom of God is near. Repent and believe the good news!"[71]

If you confess with your mouth, "Jesus is Lord," and believe in your heart that God raised him from the dead, you will be saved. For it is with your heart that you believe and are justified, and it is with your mouth that you confess and are saved. As the Scripture says, "Anyone who trusts in him will never be put to shame."[72]

---

[69] Injil - John 3:16-17
[70] Injil - John 5:24
[71] Injil - Mark 1:15
[72] Injil - Romans 10:10-11

Discussion Questions

1. Has your understanding of Isa changed since reading this chapter? If so, how?

2. Isa claimed to be the bread of life. What does that mean?

3. Which of the claims Isa made about himself is most significant or interesting to you? Why?

4. What aspect of Isa's character mentioned in this chapter do you admire the most? Why?

5. What does it mean to be a follower of Isa?

6. Do you want to be a follower of Isa?